GARFIELD
ON THE TOWN

BY: JIM DAVIS
and Lorenzo Music

ℛℛ
RAVETTE BOOKS

This edition first published by Ravette Books Limited 1987.
Reprinted 1988, 1989, 1991, 1993.

Printed and bound for Ravette Books Limited,
8 Clifford Street, London W1X 1RB
An Egmont Company
by Proost International Bookproduction, Belgium

ISBN: 0 948456 48 5

GARFIELD
ON THE TOWN

WELL, I GUESS I'LL GET UP, WAKE JON AND EXERCISE

UNLESS, OF COURSE, THAT FLOOR IS COLD

I HATE COLD FLOORS

I'M NOT GETTING OUT OF BED IF THAT FLOOR IS THE SLIGHTEST BIT CHILLY

YIIII! IT'S FREEZING!

BOYS, BOYS, BOYS. JUST LOOK AT THIS ROOM

WHAT AM I GOING TO DO WITH YOU TWO? CRUELTY TO ANIMALS COMES TO MIND...

A ONE WAY TICKET TO THE CITY POUND SEEMS LIKE A GOOD IDEA

THE VET!

DR. WILSON

WILSON

HI, DOC, THIS IS JON ARBUCKLE, YOU KNOW, GARFIELD'S OWNER

GARFIELD, WHAT NOW?

WELL, HE'S BEEN GONE FOR A WHILE, AND I WAS AFRAID HE MIGHT HAVE BEEN HIT BY A CAR

IN THAT CASE, YOU WANT A TOW TRUCK

WELL, THANKS FOR YOUR CONCERN

BOY, IT'S STARTING TO GET DARK. NO SWEAT, I CAN TAKE CARE OF MYSELF. IN FACT IT MIGHT BE KIND OF FUN TO GET INTO A LITTLE RUMBLE JUST TO LOOSEN UP

JUST LET SOMEONE TRY SOMETHING. I'LL GIVE 'EM THE OL'... HI-YA!

NOW I REMEMBER EVERYTHING

LET THE GAME BEGIN!

WHAT DO YOU WANT?

LARDBALL!

THEY WANT SOMEONE CALLED, "LARDBALL"

LARDBALL?

WHO'S LARDBALL?

GARFIELD, IS THAT YOU?

THANK YOU... THAT WAS ENOUGH FUN FOR ONE DAY

LASAGNA!

HOME, JON

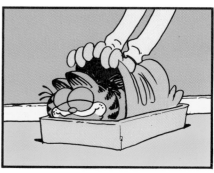

THANKS, MOM... FOR EVERYTHING

A selection of Garfield books published by Ravette

Garfield Colour TV Specials

Here Comes Garfield	£2.95
Garfield In The Rough	£2.95
Garfield In Disguise	£2.95
Garfield Goes To Hollywood	£2.95
A Garfield Christmas	£2.95
Garfield's Thanksgiving	£2.95
Garfield In Paradise	£2.95
Garfield's Feline Fantasies	£2.95
Garfield Gets A Life	£2.95

The Second Garfield Treasury	£5.95
The Third Garfield Treasury	£5.95
The Fourth Garfield Treasury	£5.95
The Fifth Garfield Treasury	£5.95
Garfield Weekend Away	£4.95
Garfield Book of Cat Names	£2.50
Garfield Best Ever	£4.85
Garfield The Easter Bunny	£3.95
Garfield How To Party	£3.95
Garfield Selection	£5.96
Garfield His 9 Lives	£5.95
The Garfield Diet Book	£4.95
The Garfield Exercise Book	£4.95

Garfield Pocket books

No. 1 Garfield The Great Lover	£2.50
No. 2 Garfield Why Do You Hate Mondays?	£2.50
No. 3 Garfield Does Pooky Need You?	£2.50
No. 4 Garfield Admit It Odie's OK!	£2.50
No. 5 Garfield Two's Company	£2.50
No. 6 Garfield What's Cooking?	£2.50
No. 7 Garfield Who's Talking?	£2.50
No. 8 Garfield Strikes Again	£2.50
No. 9 Garfield Here's Looking At You	£2.50
No. 10 Garfield We Love You Too	£2.50
No. 11 Garfield Here We Go Again	£2.50
No. 12 Garfield Life and Lasagne	£2.50
No. 13 Garfield In The Pink	£2.50
No. 14 Garfield Just Good Friends	£2.50
No. 15 Garfield Plays It Again	£2.50
No. 16 Garfield Flying High	£2.50
No. 17 Garfield On Top Of The World	£2.50
No. 18 Garfield Happy Landings	£2.50
No. 19 Garfield Going Places	£2.50
No. 20 Garfield Le Magnifique	£2.50
No. 21 Garfield In The Fast Lane	£2.50
No. 22 Garfield In Tune	£2.50
No. 23 Garfield The Reluctant Romeo	£2.50
No. 24 Garfield With Love From Me To You	£2.50
No. 25 Garfield A Gift For You	£2.50
No. 26 Garfield Great Impressions	£2.50

All these books are available at your local bookshop or newsagent, or can be ordered direct from the publisher. Just tick the titles you require and fill in the form below. Prices and availability subject to change without notice.

Ravette Books, P.O. Box 11, Falmouth, Cornwall, TR10 9EN.
Please send a cheque or postal order for the value of the book, and add the following for postage and packing:
UK including BFPO — £1.00 per order. OVERSEAS, including EIRE — £2.00 per order.
OR Please debit this amount from my Access/Visa Card (delete as appropriate).

CARD NUMBER ☐☐☐☐☐☐☐☐☐☐☐☐☐☐☐

AMOUNT £ . . . . EXPIRY DATE . . . . SIGNED . . . .

NAME . . . . ADDRESS . . . .

. . . .